FISHING

FOR FUN!

By Eric Murray

Content Adviser: Nathan Benson, BASS/ESPN Outdoors, Lake Buena Vista, Florida
Reading Adviser: Frances J. Bonacci, Ed.D, Reading Specialist, Cambridge, Massachusetts

COMPASS POINT BOOKS

MINNEAPOLIS, MINNESOTA

Compass Point Books
3109 West 50th Street, #115
Minneapolis, MN 55410

Visit Compass Point Books on the Internet at www.compasspointbooks.com
or e-mail your request to custserv@compasspointbooks.com

Photographs ©: Royalty-free/Corbis (left) front cover, (center) 10-11, Istockphoto (right) front cover, (top) 11,19; AP Wide World Photos, 4-5, 14-15, 20-21, 26-27, 35, 38-39, 40-41; Corel, 6-7, 32-33, 34, (center, right) 43, (top) 45, (right) 45; Photodisc, 8-9, 12-13, 18-19 (center), 28-29, 42-43 (background), 42 (right); Shutterstock (top) 10, 17, 24-25, 36-37; Photos.com (bottom) 10, (bottom) 11, 22-23, 30-31; Larry Hirshkowitz/Corbis, 16-17; Ingram Publishing (left) 42, Digital Stock (left) 43, (right) 44, 47; Artville, (bottom) 44-45

Editors: Deb Berry and Aubrey Whitten/Bill SMITH STUDIO; and Shelly Lyons
Designer/Page Production: Geron Hoy, Kavita Ramchandran, Sinae Sohn, Marina Terletsky, and Brock Waldron/Bill SMITH STUDIO
Photo Researcher: Jacqueline Lissy Brustein, Scott Rosen, and Allison Smith/Bill SMITH STUDIO
Art Director: Jaime Martens
Creative Director: Keith Griffin
Editorial Director: Carol Jones
Managing Editor: Catherine Neitge

Library of Congress Cataloging-in-Publication Data
Murray, Eric.
 Fishing for fun! / by Eric Murray.
   p. cm. — (For fun!)
 Includes bibliographical references and index.
 ISBN 0-7565-1684-6 (hard cover)
 1. Fishing—Juvenile literature. I. Title. II. Series.
 SH445.M87 2005
 799.1—dc22   2005030280

Printed in the United States of America.

Table of Contents

The Basics

Doing It

People, Places, and Fun

Note: In this book, there are two kinds of vocabulary words. Fishing Words to Know are words specific to fishing. They are defined on page 46. Other Words to Know are helpful words that aren't related only to fishing. They are defined on page 47.

Let's Go Fishing!

You don't have to ask too many people what their favorite way to spend an afternoon is before someone will say, "Going fishing!"

Fishing is a hobby that combines relaxation and excitement. It's a great way to enjoy time outside and be on or near the water.

Whether it's throwing out a line at your favorite pond, fly fishing in a river, or casting a line from a boat on the ocean, there's a style for everyone. So, grab your rod and reel, and let's go fishing!

What's Your Angle?
"Angling" means fishing with a hook and a line.

Quality Time

Fishing is a great way to spend time with friends or family. In between the excitement of hooking a catch, you can spend the time enjoying each other's company.

A Link to the Past

Throughout history, fishing has been more a means of gathering food than a fun way to pass time.

People have been fishing for thousands of years. The oldest known painting of an angler comes from Egypt, and it dates to about 2000 B.C.

Fishing is mentioned in the writings of the Greek philosophers Plato and Aristotle. The first book in English about fishing was written in 1496 by a nun, Dame Juliana Berners. It describes the construction of hooks and rods. It also describes how to tie knots in fishing lines, and how to make and use artificial lures and flies to attract game fish.

In 1888, men in Bala Falls, Ontario, fished to provide food for their families and to enjoy nature.

Something for Everyone

There are almost as many methods of fishing as there are fish to catch. A few of the main varieties of freshwater and saltwater fishing include:

Fly fishing (freshwater): Fly fishing is a popular method of freshwater fishing, used mostly on moving waters like rivers and streams. Trout is the most popular catch. It's called fly fishing because the lures are made to look like the flies and other insects that freshwater fish feed on.

Ice fishing (freshwater): Ice fishing doesn't require a lot of equipment. A hole is cut in the surface of a frozen lake or river, and a baited line is dipped into the hole.

Bait fishing (freshwater): Bait fishing is another popular method. When bait fishing, an angler chooses from a selection of bait and lures to attract fish. The next time you're in a tackle shop, take a look at all the lures in different sizes and colors. The largemouth bass is popular for bait fishing.

Shallow water fishing (saltwater): Small bays and coves are good places to fish in saltwater. Flounder and fluke are likely catches.

Deep-sea fishing (saltwater): You need a boat for deep-sea fishing. It can be the most exciting way to fish. All of the large fish, like marlin, are in very deep ocean waters.

Getting Started

So you want to go fishing? Well, you'll need some basic equipment to get started.

Rod and reel: The rod you choose depends on the type of fishing you want to try. Generally, there are three types of rods: bait-casting, spinning, and fly fishing. The easiest way to start is with a bait casting rod. There are several inexpensive beginner's kits on the market. They come with a rod and reel.

Tackle box: You're going to need a place to keep your lures, spare hooks, bobbers, and tackle. Tackle boxes are tool boxes for anglers. They come in different sizes and colors and have separate storage compartments.

Lures or bait: Of course, you aren't going to catch anything if there's nothing on the end of your line that a fish would want to eat. The type of fish you are trying to catch will determine whether you use live bait or lures.

Fishing License

You might need a fishing license to fish legally. Fees from fishing licenses go toward conservation and clean water programs, fish restocking, and youth-oriented programs to promote fishing. So, aside from being legal, you're promoting the sport!

The Bait Debate

Which one to use, bait or lure? It depends on what type of fish you are trying to catch. Anglers already familiar with your fishing spot will be a good source of information, but here are some guidelines:

Bait: Fishing with bait means that you are using a fish's natural food source (or something that looks and acts like it) to attract the fish to your hook. Common "live" baits are earthworms, minnows, fly larvae, grasshoppers, and crickets. Cast with a softer touch when using live bait. You don't want the bait to fly off of the hook. The downside of live bait is that you generally only get one cast out of it. And don't jerk the line around too much while trying to attract a fish, or you could lose the bait.

Lures: Lures are useful because they can be used over and over again. They come in thousands of shapes, sizes, and colors. The important thing about a lure is this: It should look or move like a fish, or like something a fish would eat. Because a lure is tied securely to the end of your line, you can cast it much farther than with live bait. When buying a lure, ask how deep it runs, what kind of movement it has, and how fast it moves. These qualities depend on the type of fish the lure was designed to catch.

Choosing the Right Rod for You

Fishing rods are made out of graphite, or a mixture of graphite and fiberglass. Graphite is a light but very strong material. It is also inexpensive. There are three main types of fishing rods.

Spinning rods: This rod is used by beginners and experienced anglers. They can use heavy lures or lighter lures like flies.

Fly rods: Fly rods are used by more experienced anglers. Fly fishing requires a more specific technique for casting and isn't recommended for beginners.

Bait-casting rods: These rods are designed to deliver heavier weights than spinning and fly rods. They are good to use with large, heavy lures or live bait.

Grip: It's where you hang on for dear life when you've got a big one on the line! The grip should feel comfortable in your hands.

Guides: The guides direct the line as it comes off the reel to the tip top of the rod.

Butt: The bottom half of the rod.

Tip: The last foot of the rod. Depending on how stiff the fishing rod is, it may bend a little or a lot.

Tip Top: The point where the line leaves the rod.

Lure Them In

There are thousands of lures on the market, but they are all variations on a few tried-and-true types of lures.

Plugs: A plug is a type of lure that looks like a fish. Variations on plug lures include poppers, deep divers, chuggers, and jerkbaits. These names come from the type of motion they generate.

Spoons: Spoon lures are made of flat, shiny pieces of metal. Long ago, people used spoons with fish hooks attached to them. Variations of spoon lures are spinners, spinnerbaits, and jigs.

Plastic Worms

The plastic worm is the most popular type of lure. They are inexpensive and work with almost all fishing techniques. There is an endless variety of sizes and colors of plastic worms.

It's a Live One!

If you want to use live bait, you're going to have to stick a hook through a big night crawler! It seems gross, but it's a part of the sport, and eventually you get used to it.

There are three basic methods:

The easiest way is to push the hook through the collar of the worm. It is the smooth section near the middle of the worm.

Another way to hook a worm is to put the point of the hook through the worm's head, and then out through the collar. This will cause the worm to have lifelike movement as it goes through the water.

The third method is called Texas rigging. The hook goes through the head of the worm, and then is turned so the point goes into the collar. This prevents the worm from getting caught in the weeds while being reeled in.

Do Worms Feel Pain When You Hook Them?
Scientists believe that because of their simple nervous systems, invertebrates (worms), like night crawlers, do not feel pain the same way humans do.

Basics of Casting a Line

You've found a spot and baited your hook. Now it's time to get that bait in front of a fish. After all, they aren't going to just jump into the boat! It's time to cast your line into the water.

Let's assume you have a beginner's spin-casting rod and reel. This reel has a push-button release that lets out the line. This type of rod is the easiest to cast.

With your thumb resting on the button, point your shoulder at your target area (left shoulder if you are left-handed, right shoulder otherwise).

Point the rod at the target at a 45 degree angle, and then quickly bring the rod back to an upright position. Once the rod is straight, stop the backstroke, then begin the forward stroke.

When the rod comes forward to about 40 degrees, push the release button and stop the forward motion. The weight of the lure will carry the line toward your target.

When it reaches the target, take your thumb off of the release button. This will stop the line from unspooling any further, and you can begin working the bait or lure as you reel in the line. The motions you use to make the bait appear lifelike will vary, depending on what you are using. If you reel all of the line in without a bite, it's time to cast again.

Rod and Reel

You feel a tug on the line, and you yank the rod back as hard as you can. The only problem is the fish isn't there anymore. This is the hard part—setting the hook and reeling it in.

When you feel the fish take your lure or bait, drop the rod tip.

Once you feel that the bait is in the fish's mouth, reel in any slack in the line, and then lift the rod high and with force to embed the hook in your catch's mouth.

Hold the rod at an angle that allows it to remain bent. This will put continuous pressure on the fish, eventually causing it to get tired. You can bring in the fish by dropping the rod, reeling in line, and then pulling back the rod again. Repeat this process until you are ready to land the fish.

Once you have the fish next to the boat or near the shore, you or a friend can use a net to pull the fish from the water. If you aren't keeping the fish, remove the hook while the fish is in the net. This way, you can prevent any further trauma to the fish, releasing it back into the water.

Rules to Fish By

Depending on where you are fishing, there may be local rules that limit the amount of fish you can keep. If everybody caught as many fish as they could, the stocks of available fish would decrease. This could unbalance the environment of the fish, causing dramatic changes in the local food chain.

There is a popular concept among anglers that all beginners should follow. It's called the principle of catch and release. Unless you are fishing for food or catch a really big fish that could set a record, it's a good idea to gently release the fish back into the water.

The small fish that you didn't intend to keep could go back and have babies, which could make that spot even better for fishing in the future. That little fish you released might grow up to be a real whopper!

Be a Good Sport

Practicing the catch and release philosophy protects the sport of fishing for everyone.

The One That Didn't Get Away!

Every now and then, you might land a fish that's bigger than you ever caught before. It's a great idea to always have a camera with you so you can have a record of your biggest catches. Have a friend take a picture of you with your prized catch, and then get it back into the water as soon as you can.

Very rarely, you may catch a fish that's big enough to be a record breaker. As you become a more experienced angler, keep a scale with you so you can weigh your fish. If you happen to catch a record-breaking fish, you might want to take it to a taxidermist to preserve and mount the fish as a trophy. Here are some tips on what to do if that happens:

- Take a picture first. This will help the taxidermist preserve the fish in a more lifelike state.

- Cover the fish with a wet cloth, laying it as flat as you can, and then store it in a cooler full of ice.

- If you are close to home, try to get the fish frozen as quickly as you can. Seal the fish in a plastic bag, make sure most of the air is out of the bag, and lay the fish flat.

- The sooner you get the fish to a taxidermist, the better your results will be.

- Pick out a nice spot on your wall to display your trophy!

Taxidermy

Taxidermy is a general term describing the many methods of preserving a lifelike representation of an animal.

Keeping It Safe

Remember that while fishing can be fun and relaxing, it can also be dangerous. Fish hooks are sharp and can do a lot of damage. So be extra careful.

Always look before you cast to see if there is anything or anyone behind you.

If your line gets caught in a tree, never try yanking it toward you. Should the hook come free, it could fly toward you and injure you or someone nearby.

If you're fishing from a boat, always wear a life jacket. Fishing on a boat can be awkward if you've never done it before, and it's easy to lose your balance and fall if you aren't paying attention.

If you can't get the line free by gently tugging on it, accept the loss of your lure or bait and cut the line.

Lastly, you're going to be out in the sun, so use plenty of sunblock to prevent sunburn. A bad sunburn can ruin many days of good fishing.

The Best Fishing on Earth

There are several places in the world where the excitement of fishing is unmatched. Depending on what you're fishing for, you may find yourself in Canada, Australia, South America, or in the middle of the Pacific Ocean. Here are a few examples of some of the best fishing spots in the world:

British Columbia, Canada: The lakes, rivers, and saltwaters of western Canada provide amazing sportfishing. British Columbia is a beautiful place to fish for trout, salmon, or halibut.

Costa Rica: This beautiful country has many charter boats to take you on fishing adventures. Typical deep sea catches include marlin, sailfish, and tuna. Some tuna caught in Costa Rica have weighed more than 350 pounds (158 kg).

The Bahamas: Fishing is one of the best reasons to go to these Caribbean islands. The flats and deep waters of the Bahamas are suitable for beginners and for sportfishing enthusiasts.

The Caribbean is a good place to catch many types of fish.

Fishing for Life

Some people fish for a living. Careers in the fishing industry range from ordinary to life-threatening! Here are a few examples:

Fishing guide: A guide is a person who amateur anglers can hire for a day to show them how to improve their skills. Guides show novice anglers how to properly and safely use the tools of the trade. They also introduce new anglers to prime fishing locations. Guides may take anglers out to sea for deep sea fishing or to a lake for fresh air and clear waters.

Fish and game warden: Fish and game wardens work for the U.S. government. They provide information and protect natural resources. Wardens can be thought of as nature police, but the only time you're likely to encounter one while fishing is when they are checking for valid fishing licenses.

Most of the fish you eat at home or at school is caught by commercial fishermen.

Commercial fishing: Commercial fishing is often called the most dangerous job in the world. It is done for profit, not for fun. However, the people who do it for a living often speak of how much they love their job, about being out on the open sea, and having a sense of freedom. They do this despite working with dangerous, heavy equipment, like massive nets and hydraulic winches, sometimes in very bad weather and rough seas.

Fishing for Fame and Fortune

Fishing tournaments keep getting more popular every year, with the top competitors gaining fame, prizes, and lots of televison coverage. Some anglers have so many sponsor logos on their outfits that they are beginning to look like race car drivers!

All fishing tournaments have rules. They vary somewhat, based on the location of the tournament and the type of fish you are trying to catch, but several rules are almost always the same:

- There is usually a limit on how many fish you can catch. Some tournaments make you release your biggest catch if you go over the limit.

- The fish have to come in at a minimum weight or length in order to qualify for judging.

- There are usually restrictions on where you can cast your lines to catch fish for the tournament.

- There is a time limit on how long you can be out fishing before you have to come back for the weigh-in.

In all cases, state laws must be followed and participants must have licenses to fish. It pays to know the rules if you fish a tournament.

International Fishing Economies

For most people, fishing is a relaxing pastime, but for some, fishing is still a means of survival. In some areas, families have relied on fishing as a way to provide food and income for generations, sometimes selling their daily catch at local markets.

Some people fish the coastlines with handmade nets called cast nets. They are used for harvesting smaller types of fish that can be used for both food and bait for larger fish.

Others use the same techniques as recreational anglers do, except they keep what they catch. The methods used are the same, but instead of bringing home a photograph to treasure, they bring home dinner for the family.

Nets can be used to catch large schools of fish that can provide food and income for many days.

Catch of the Century

So you want to know about world record fish? Read about these beauties!

Giant catfish: On May 1, 2005, fishermen in northern Thailand caught a fish as big as a grizzly bear. A 646-pound (291 kg) Mekong giant catfish was the heaviest recorded since Thai officials started keeping records in 1981.

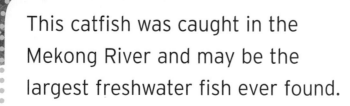

This catfish was caught in the Mekong River and may be the largest freshwater fish ever found.

Atlantic blue marlin: The world record Atlantic blue marlin was caught in Vitoria, Brazil, on February 29, 1992, by Paulo R.A. Amorim. It weighed in at an astounding 1,402 pounds and 2 ounces (631 kg)!

Largest fish ever: The largest fish ever caught was a whale shark, captured in the Gulf of Thailand in 1919. The whale shark was more than 59 feet (18 m) long! The whale shark is considered the largest species of fish. Normal adults often grow to be 45 feet (14 m) long and can weigh up to 15 tons!

Sun and Saltwater

Pier fishing, as you might have guessed by the name, is fishing from a pier. It's very popular for people who live near an ocean.

Most coastal communities, such as those in California, Florida, and New England, have plenty of piers for fishing. It is a great way to enjoy saltwater fishing without getting on a boat. Many piers are long and stretch out to parts of the water that are deep enough to attract some really big fish. Plus, there's no better place to watch a beautiful sunset than from a pier!

A Legendary Pier

One of the most famous piers in the country is the Steeplechase Pier in Coney Island, New York. The pier was built in 1897 and stretches 700 feet (214 m) from the boardwalk into the Atlantic Ocean!

What Happened When?

1195   1400   1600   1700   1800   1900

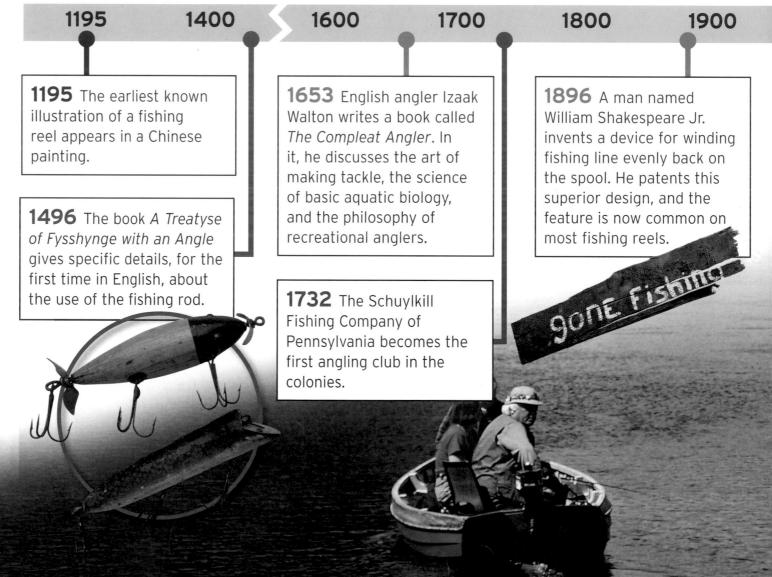

1195 The earliest known illustration of a fishing reel appears in a Chinese painting.

1496 The book *A Treatyse of Fysshynge with an Angle* gives specific details, for the first time in English, about the use of the fishing rod.

1653 English angler Izaak Walton writes a book called *The Compleat Angler*. In it, he discusses the art of making tackle, the science of basic aquatic biology, and the philosophy of recreational anglers.

1732 The Schuylkill Fishing Company of Pennsylvania becomes the first angling club in the colonies.

1896 A man named William Shakespeare Jr. invents a device for winding fishing line evenly back on the spool. He patents this superior design, and the feature is now common on most fishing reels.

gone Fishing

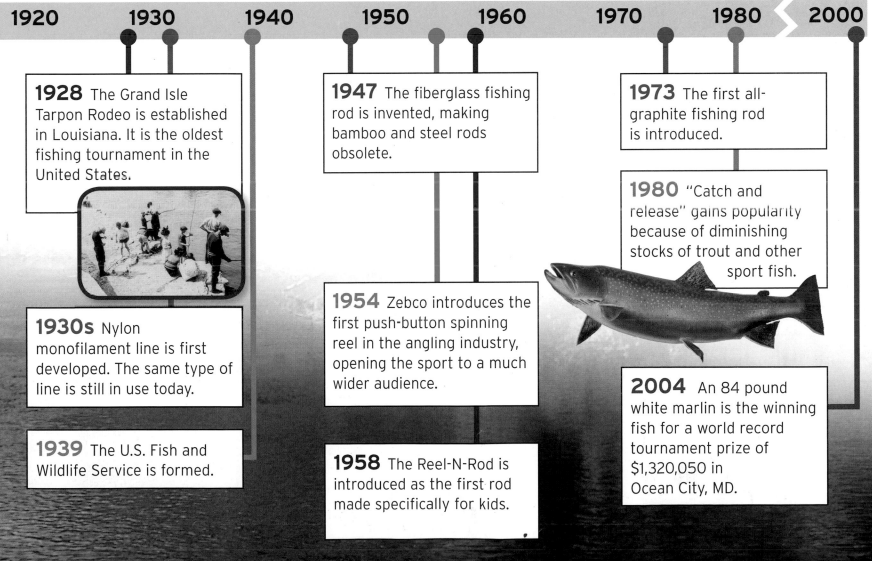

1920   **1930**   **1940**   **1950**   **1960**   **1970**   **1980**   **2000**

1928 The Grand Isle Tarpon Rodeo is established in Louisiana. It is the oldest fishing tournament in the United States.

1947 The fiberglass fishing rod is invented, making bamboo and steel rods obsolete.

1973 The first all-graphite fishing rod is introduced.

1980 "Catch and release" gains popularity because of diminishing stocks of trout and other sport fish.

1930s Nylon monofilament line is first developed. The same type of line is still in use today.

1954 Zebco introduces the first push-button spinning reel in the angling industry, opening the sport to a much wider audience.

1939 The U.S. Fish and Wildlife Service is formed.

1958 The Reel-N-Rod is introduced as the first rod made specifically for kids.

2004 An 84 pound white marlin is the winning fish for a world record tournament prize of $1,320,050 in Ocean City, MD.

Fun Fishing Facts

Bass will often strike at a lure right after being released because they have two memory centers—one for each eye. A bass might hit your lure the first time because he sees it from his left eye. If he shakes it loose, he might hit it again after seeing it with his right eye!

The fastest fish in the world is the sailfish, which has been clocked at 68 miles (109 km) per hour.

The world's slowest fish is the seahorse. Smaller species like the dwarf seahorse never attain speeds of more than 0.001 miles (.0016 km) per hour.

Fishing is one of the few outdoor sports you can participate in at any time of the year.

Fishing ranks as the fourth most popular participation sport in the nation. It ranks ahead of basketball, baseball, soccer, and football! Only walking, swimming, and camping are more popular.

Some fish burrow in the sandy bottom or hide in crevices to rest. Other fish can't sleep—they need to keep swimming in order to breathe.

The dwarf goby is the smallest marine fish and is believed to be the smallest vertebrate in the world. Mature females reach only .32 to .4 inches (8 to 10 mm) or the size of a pumpkin seed in length!

Flying fish do not really fly, but they can glide on air up to 1/4 mile (0.4 km) with their outstretched wings.

Fishing Words to Know

angling: fishing for enjoyment, catching one fish at a time using a hook

aquatic: having to do with water

barb: the spur found on the point of most fish hooks

bait: food or other lure placed on a hook and used for catching fish

cast: to throw out a lure or bait at the end of a fishing line

catch and release: angling for fish and releasing them back immediately

food chain: the chain of organisms in a community that produce food and consume it

game fish: fish that are caught for sport

habitat: the area where organisms live

invertebrate: an animal (such as a worm) that does not have a backbone

life vest: personal flotation device to be worn while boating to keep a person afloat if thrown overboard

lure: any artificial bait used to attract and catch fish

reel: a cylinder or spool that is used to wind and unwind fishing line

reservoir: a lakelike body of water created by damming a stream or river

rod: a thin, straight piece or bar of material, such as metal, wood, graphite, or fiberglass

spawning: the reproductive activity of fish

stock: to populate a body of water with fish raised in hatcheries

tackle: the equipment used in a particular activity, especially in fishing

taxidermist: a craftsman who stuffs and mounts the skins of animals for display

test: fishing line strength as stated on the label

Other Words to Know

ethics: concerns about what is morally right or wrong

philosophy: a set of ideas or beliefs that relate to a particular field or activity

technique: the skills, form, and basic physical movements needed for an activity

tournament: a group of contests where the person with the best record at the end is the winner

Where To Learn More

At The Library

Fabian, John. *Fishing For Beginners.* New York: Scribner, 1974.

Hansen, Chris. *Fly Fishing for Beginners (The Freshwater Angler).* Chanhassen, Minn.: Creative Publishing International, 2002.

On The Road

Catskill Fly Fishing Center and Museum
1031 Old Route 17
Livingston Manor, NY 12758

On The Web

For more information on this topic, use FactHound.

1. Go to *www.facthound.com*
2. Type in this book ID: 0756516846
3. Click on the *Fetch It* button.

FactHound will find the best Web sites for you.

INDEX

ABOUT THE AUTHOR

Eric Murray is a writer who lives in Jersey City, New Jersey. In addition to being a writer, he is an avid musician and graphic artist. His two favorite places to go fishing are the Chesapeake Bay in Maryland, and Homosassa Springs, Florida.